CW00456783

Drizzle Mizzle Downpour Deluge

Born in Swansea, Stephen Knight lives in London.

also by Stephen Knight

DRIZZLE MIZZLE
DOWNPOUR DELUGE

Stephen Knight

ACKNOWLEDGEMENTS

Times Literary Supplement, *Poetry Wales*, *London Review of Books*,
Poetry London, *Poetry Ireland Review*, The British Council's *New Writing 7*
(Vintage, 1998) and *NW14* (Granta, 2006).

First published in 2020
by CB editions
146 Percy Road London W12 9QL
www.cbeditions.com

Printed in England by Blissetts, London W3 8DH

ISBN 978–1–909585–31–7

Mae hi'n bwrw hen wragedd a ffyn

Contents

Are We There Yet?

We are travelling for ages
Though the wind and rain are frontal
Hence the windscreen wipers ticking
And my heartbeat (contrapuntal)

And the parents half in shadow
In no mood for conversation
Who have stared towards our future
Or the nearest filling station

Since we left my worn-out childhood
On the verge with neither sorrow
Nor a *Thank The Lord it's over*
Then headed for tomorrow

In this silence they are nursing
Which is blacker than it's hollow
We are many miles from somewhere
Without a map to follow

We are somewhere that is no place
In the night which makes me shiver
And the sky is made of thunder
And the road is made of river

In Which We Are Cast As Ourselves

It doesn't smell of us,
  This three-walled room
Calm, black-clothed figures
  Alter in the gloom

With Lego bricks, books,
  An unread magazine
And shoes no one wears.
  What does this mean?

The bedrooms don't exist!
  The staircase only stops.
Beyond the cyclorama?
  God knows – not shops

Nor terraced houses
  Spectral as they near
The vanishing point
  (Where nothing's clear).

Everyone else knows
  Where to stand and when
To look – I muddle
  Now and Then.

Dim the lights,
  A decade passes
And then I return
  Fatter, in glasses.

Leaving in their wake
  Columns of dusty air
– In which we linger, bright
  Beyond compare –

The children leave like
  Something dreamt
. . .
    . . .

What happens now?
  Do I make a long,
Slow exit stage right?
  Or burst into song?

Not knowing is scary!
  Not knowing is fun!
My wife agrees with me.
  She might be anyone.

Long Before THE END

                        we left our livid tip-up seats
  Another boy and me I don't know who or when
  The light on our shoulders of things still happening
Of gilded Shirley Eaton still on her hotel sheets
  And nothing whatsoever nothing to be done
  And nothing but my fear of that world
No consolation in my bag of hard-boiled sweets
  No comfort in the aisles
  Release me from this dark I might have thought
Deliver me from Technicolor death-defying feats
  The whispering the crimson curtains folded back
  Then headed home talking to no one
Uphill through brilliant ordinary streets
  On which the day still shone
  Or rained (I couldn't say)

The Golden State

for Colleen

If not the giant redwoods
taking centuries to reach
the light, nor the lights-
camera-action typhoons
regular as clockwork
in the murky Tonga Bar,
nor, perched above LA,
the penitential Getty,
nor even the *Chronicle's*
news that the universe
is flat, and expanding
faster and faster forever
– Wow! Wow! Wow!
to quote one scientist –
then how about the way
you drove your car
wrists out, double-jointed,
or, sealed in silver paper,
those skinny joints
I could never light,
or the line in a Visitors' Book
in the Valley of the Moon
left a decade earlier
(*This is a beautiful setting*
to put the ghosts to rest)
or else that 'bohemian'
legacy of Venice Beach,
a henna tendril
fading from your ankle
slowly, over days.

Yellow Notebook

Open with an open door Shoes cups a scatter of books Cast a man who looks Like no one we know Cast a man who looks Like anyone but me By the quality of light Establish early summer Open with music Admit no latecomers ~~He was out in the garden telling the bees Out past the sycamores out in the dusk Hatless and coatless with unnumbered trees Down by the ha-ha telling the bees.~~ I wanted to be good I always wanted to be good Are you singing now Have you forgotten yet That voice from another room Your brother's voice Your own woah-oh-oh yeah yeah yeah sea scrambling and crumbling the wind off the waves tastes of swimming chin-up spluttering two towels a flask a football the steps to the beach are new somewhere between here and the far shore did we forget who we were boing colour crash consume collect a beach stick by stick stone by stone Sometimes a street needs people with umbrellas Sometimes the rain has nowhere to go The one who never meets your eye The one you know is gone The one you know has gone Which one is right The one you know you know Up the bendy ladder The room has opened its heart to me Why put salt on ice why put salt in beer why pay more why pee after sex why oh why why nipple pain why network marketing why not why me lord why me why am i always tired why am i so tired We are shadows I At the edge of light I Shone for others I Night after night I Even those chairs I Downstage have more I To say than us I Even that door I Opened wide I On nothing much I Of consequence I To see or touch Olive green Meccano/slow/low This door is alarmed Roy's bench HAPPY'S bench Pej's bench Only sad things make me write

Happy Families

The vicar was a tired man whose sympathy was token.
Mourners left his side, alas, a little more heartbroken.
The sexton was the tasteful one. His furniture was oaken.
No one here has listened to a word that we have spoken.

The grasses grow as high as boys where butterflies once fluttered.
The butcher was a private man who kept his windows shuttered.
The baker wore his apron loose and liked his pancakes buttered.
No one here has listened to a word that we have uttered.

The barber lived a sheltered life, the sweep was bigger boned.
The rain itself was piteous, the wild wind always moaned.
The headstones weren't the only things the wicked weather honed.
No one here has listened to a word that we've intoned.

The grasses grow as grasses do, as someone somewhere stated.
More than simply bothersome, the doctor's shyness grated.
The milkman too was hapless. His very tread was hated.
No one here has listened to a word that we've orated.

The grasses grow as high as men where butterflies once flittered.
Some say the carpenter was mad, while others say embittered.
As for the bishop's voice: how the congregation tittered!
No one here has listened to a word that we have wittered.

The vicar was bone idle and the sexton overfed.
There hasn't been a service here since those two went to bed.
The grass between the gravestones is fuelled by the dead.
No one here has listened to a word that we have said.

The Last Bus

If anyone should know
The number of this bus
And where it means to go,
I wish they'd say.

– Each window
Fills its face with night.

At every stop, the night
Removes more passengers
From sight.
The doors hiss shut

On warmth and light
And, out there,

Something else. Out there
The town has gone,
So where
Exactly are we bound?

Our passage stirs the air.
Air settles in our wake.

~

We travel quiet streets
I do not know –
A pocketful of sweets,
Tickets on the plush

Of all the empty seats,
A satchel by my side.

The dark's outside
And I am glad of that.
I haven't cried
Aloud — not once! —

But I have tried.
You see that face?

Unlike my real face
That one belongs out there,
Lost in outer space.
— How quietly

We race
Towards our stop.

~

First, the sky was grey
And then the night
Extinguished the day.
Our driver looked

The other way.
What has he seen

That we haven't seen?
Something outside
His black windscreen
Frightens me.

Where have we been?
Where are we going?

And why are we going
Down unlit streets
– Speeding, slowing,
Stopping for others –

Without my knowing
Which stop is mine?

~

We are bound
At speed, East or West
Where night has drowned
Every thing

And every sound –
But who

Are we? And who
Looks back at us?
No one I talk to,
No one I know

Wet through
With rain.

Out there, the rain
Comes down,
Filling every drain
The silent

Citizens maintain
With steel and stone.

~

Our backsides ache
From staying put
So long. – Awake,
But only just,

We take
Comfort from doors

(Those folding doors)
Folding shut
On rain that pours
On every thing

The dark abhors.
We settle back,

Expecting no way back
From here,
Nor any cul de sac
To slow us down.

Amnesiac,
We rush headlong.

~

If we are in a state,
If our homework's lost
For ever, or late,
Our stop

Will have to wait.
Outside, it's cold.

In here, the cold
Of night and rain
Finds no hold,
Even when

The doors unfold.
But where we go

And why we go
We cannot say,
Nor will we know
At last

Why Life at first is slow
Then very fast.

My Future

– waiting for me somewhere out of sight
past the betting shop and the Nationwide
where buses stop
to shiver in the middle of the night –
doesn't for a moment doubt
we'll recognize each other
when he looks me in the eye,
but wonders if the buttonhole was wise
or lifts a wristwatch to his ear
then sighs before a table
laid with shiny cutlery and a cloth
so white
it seems to generate its own light.
The napkins' beautiful, useless folds!

Fancy Dress

the sleeves so long
you never see your thumbs
the trousers halfway up your calves
Love's a disappointing costume
its mask's one eyehole
much too small

but you stand before the mirror
saying *mmm this one will do*
folding the till receipt
neatly
           in case

The Call Box

Outside this one
A queue has formed.
It's almost warm
So someone takes
A blazer off
– How posh they look! –
And pink magnolias
Open their arms
To a breeze that stirs
Their Sunday best.
Ready to brave
The smell of piss
And a crackly line
So they can say
The word or two
They might have said
Before – if only
They had known –
They wait for hours
Rehearsing messages
Written in full
On headed paper
Or scribbled in haste
On old receipts
And kept till now
In handbags, wallets
And inside-pockets.
They jingle change.
It isn't cold.

When We Have Left the Room

our younger selves will stay
behind, haunting the blind
doorways and shelves on which we let
ash from a final cigarette
buckle in the crash.

        (Then, the flies begin
        knocking on doors
        the spiders spin,
        and rust explores.)

        Still, they're happy
        where they are,
        the boys and girls
        we were – waiting
        patiently as books.
Abandoned there for good,
they make no noise.
              – Well,
nothing we can hear.

Where This Train Terminates

The world is packed with scaffolding and empty packing-crates
Where this train terminates
The humid air is poorly when the clouds are working nights
Moths crowd the windows dreaming hard of cancelled flights

Where this train terminates
Waiters ghost among the tables clearing dinner plates
Cocky foxes wearing human stoles take in the sights
Shadows build in places theirs by rights

The PM's in a rocking-chair and the Chancellor is Norman Bates
Where this train terminates
Wings and beaks admire us from uncontested heights
The dead are using Twitter which amuses as it bites

Vox populi on Channel 4 dismays the Darwinites
The last ones out alas put out the pilot-lights
Then Life brings down the metal shutters and locks the metal gates
And this train terminates

2016

Rail Replacement Bus Service

We wait behind the yellow line.
The tannoy diagnoses countless ills.
The wind along the platform chills.
The trains that stop are never mine!

Only the hopeless disembark.
All day, the sun – before the sun went down –
Smeared its light all over town.
Behind the yellow line, it's dark.

Behind the yellow line, it's late.
The southbound birds have given up their songs.
The night is where the night belongs.
Buckets and mops procrastinate.

Behind the yellow line, it rains.
It rains enough to build a biggish sea.
The rainfall only falls on me.
The tannoy up above explains,

Inaudibly, the long delay
In words both crackly and grey
To those who should or should not stay.
The yellow line will never say.

Helma Lydia Knight
née Mödritscher

Tell me, what is it you plan to do
with your one wild and precious life?

– Mary Oliver, 'The Summer Day'

My mother is dead and so are you
six days apart as it happens/happened
and there's an end to Pulitzers and Guggenheims
and my mother's unease
and the Warfarin and the Venlafaxine
and the CT scans and the ERCPs
and the feeding tube

let the soft animal of your body
love what it loves   'Wild Geese'
    the walking-frame the empty hours
    the footstool and the slippers
    beside her orthopaedic chair
    the trivial bloodspots and food stains
    there and there
        the vase of knitted flowers
    the bouquet of old umbrellas
        the birdseed on the sills
    with a view of a wall of evergreens
        and the sea just out of sight

too neat for a Trümmerfilm
    but almost as grim

her ready meals mushed
    a diet of TV chefs all day
and something worse
all night

21

faced with this pabulum
who wouldn't look glum

but thank you Isla Dewar
for *Giving Up On Ordinary*
thank you Lily Baxter
for *We'll Meet Again*
so long Bash the cleaner's
nip of disinfectant in the air
farewell the physio
another Mary and Pam
the hairdresser goodbye
the friendly chiropodist
and the man from Baywash
whose name I never knew
thank you thank you
thank you

no more buses to one
confused hospital or another
around the houses and past The Liberty
home of the relegated Swans
no more grey-haired children
looking left then right
then wandering the floors
as if they had never
visited the place before
Oh sweetness pure and simple,
may I join you?   'The Roses'
with grapes or bananas
trousers knickers tops
so many nightgowns
past High Street Station
Base-Rite Scaffolding
Jesus Is Alive
my mother is not

patter shower cloudburst plash
  seldom shoures soote
but rain on this bleak hut
  drizzle mizzle downpour deluge
so coldly so straightly
such arrows of rain
  not rain to lave the drouths
but rain
possessing her entirely the twilight and the rain
  the wakeful rainy nights
the rain it raineth every day
  it rained and the wind was never weary
it rained in her heart
  nothing it seemed could survive the flood
often Cataracts and Hyrricano's
  somewhere becoming rain
but never Gene Kelly's
doodle oo doo
doodle doodle doo
doody

my mother, alas, alas,
did not always love her life

the rainfall placed her tablets
on a flower-patterned saucer

beside a glass of water

the rainfall's fingers shook
with psychotropic drugs

I cut the rainfall's fingernails

having fallen the rainfall passed
one night on the kitchen floor

the rainfall bruised easily

I swore in the rainfall's face
I raised a hand to the rainfall

then hid behind this metaphor

but every Christmas tinsel in Oma's hair
and bunny ears one Easter in her seventies

before that all-but-silent ghost of the wards
how suddenly violent my mother was
  as changeable as weather
before her housebound fear of the knock on the door
  what a Penthesilea
moody and magnificent to quote my father
and also blunt she asked me aged fifteen
are you masturbating yet

Mary does writing an elegy count

Hello, sun in my face
Hello, you who make the morning 'Why I Wake Early'

  how she turned all day
the earth of two allotments
  with seldom a break
a child of the *Anschluss*
  more likely to give than take
spuds flowers lettuces
  left on doorsteps before the dawn
not a Ceres but a Proserpina rather
stolen away by my bewildered father
  how like the snow the sun
the noisy nosey rain
  she fell on everything
and everyone
  how much of her
there was

let's say what's left of a fire
circled with tins and bottles
just out of reach of the tide
and footprints leading away
and the smallest of waves
and the softest of breezes
and the blank page of the shore

A poem should always have birds in it   'Singapore'
then birds OK that flew this far
for nothing that wasn't here before

unvergesslich bleibst du uns
pfiat di, liebe Heli

'she swam in the freezing sea'
'she wore a flowered swimming cap'
'she grew the best beans'

stick

thát

in

your

pipe

and

smoke

it

Mary

Oliver

i.m.

Hamelin

toy cars and kites crayons trodden in the earth
jigsaw pieces seasoning the path

train sets and hula hoops shed in stages
fragments of their comics caught in hedges

following the music like a doughnut smell
here is where they left shoes that grew too small

little plastic elephants and hippopotamuses
lions tigers someone somewhere misses

I could not tell you now how glad they were
heading out like conscripts off to war

goodbye goodbye goodbye they didn't look
no final glance no turning back

humming singing dancing in the open spaces
the last to go with smiles like melon slices

Swimming for Beginners

Dad, we've been forgotten.
The sky remains the sky,
The shore no different than it was before,
And when you were alive
The sand poured like this through my open hand . . .
But I place a towel here
And then turn round,
Shielding my eyes against the sun
Because the tide is too far out for us to see.
So, off we go together,
You leading me.
– And finally our footprints join us
When we near the water's edge
(Which, as I fear,
Looks anything but blue).

Echolalia Park

Hug your briefcase like you love it on the slide.
Shout WHEE, but mind your elbows on the side
The whole way down. Bigger boys than you have cried.
If they tell you otherwise, they will have lied.

Chair a very important meeting on the swings.
Keep on swinging even when your iPhone rings.
Explain that you are busiest with other things
Then see what kind of day the weather brings.

Don't be scared. Being grown up is a stupid game.
Sling your tie and jacket on the climbing-frame.
Answer to shouts of Twat or Prickface free of shame.
No one out here calls you by your proper name!

Look up at that blue and not a single cloud.
Do things that would not make your parents proud
And then say anything to please the crowd.
You will never be this big again, or loud.

Wear football boots if you want, even if it's dry
And ask, 'Why shouldn't I?' if someone asks you why
Or else stick out your bottom lip and offer no reply
Or yell FUCK OFF then make them cry.

Could any other afternoon be quite so sweet?
One team photograph and the day will be complete –
Your hands so filthy, your hair no longer neat,
Your arms around your pals, the world at your feet.

A Night Out

for Katy

An archaeologist
could reconstruct
the evening, stage

by stage, from this –
a crumpled towel

drying on the floor;
a nebula of talc;
and, in the sink,

the tiniest amount
of powdered hair.

~

Left, then right foot
up, against the basin,
you shave your legs.

The razor's buzzing
pesters the house.

The water's running.
On its shelf, our wild
asparagus fern drops

star-shaped blossom
small as crumbs.

~

Suds and flowers brush
The taps, the overflow,
your polished skin.

You ease your body
under with a sigh.

The occasional
plop of the soap
opens your eyes.

Curlicues of steam.
Bubbles popping.

~

Late (as usual!)
you rub a porthole
on the mirror: peer.

The towel falls
around your ankles.

Mascara. Blusher.
Wristwatch. Clothes.
One last look. Yes.

In a moment
you'll be gone.

1995

The Finishing Touch

for Oliver Reynolds

The man who steadies the wooden ladder
    – though steadying is not required –
looks from side to side
                            he's looking tired
        more tired than the man above
singing-stroke-humming of sadness and love
with sadness of love
                            in love with sadness
        no lovelorn mood unsung

        careful to the point of madness
his right foot planted on the bottom rung
        our man below looks sadder
because there's always damage to repair

        a mighty midday sun is shining
on one man busy the other pining
        hm hm hm the lights down low

        2 brushes   a hammer   3 pots of paint
something taking shape or looking better
        cleaner   sturdier   then that faint
        outline of
                            a face?   a letter?
initials perhaps
                        proof they were there

As I Live and Breathe

I met our old home by The Albert
Of all those years ago last night –
The stairs up, the red front door no longer red,
The golden chain tree waiting for its moment.
The place was distant, but polite.

Our maisonette! You would have known it anywhere,
On the same corner as if nothing had changed,
But no lights on. Perhaps we were asleep.
(What did we ever dream up there,
Folded in that velvet dark our curtains made?)

I would have loved to look inside, to see
The absences: those little flowers on the wall,
That chessboard lino in the hall.
– But here they are, in words instead,
As real as they will ever be.

Orpheus. Eurydice. Hermes

Rilke | Hardy

'Twas there the Shades dwelt: underground,
      Far underground;
Engulphing silence all around.
      Thuswise, yon three upclomb
Amidst the dearest dust and bones –
The man; the One who chaperones;
And late-lamented her – 'twixt red-veined stones,
      To fetch his Heartmate home.

Benighted purlieus robed in mist
      Wherein (he wist)
Not dead nor living lovers tryst –
      All things thereat were grey
And cold as any lake, and still:
Forests; bridges over naught but ill;
Drear leazes; ay, and one pale path uphill
      Whereon he led the way.

~

Along that road
He quicker strode
Than any fearful wight –
Like one quite dead
He stared ahead
Toward a distant light.

His tread did maul
That path withal,
The lyre hung by his side.
  – He wist not when
He might again
Its dol'rous airs abide.

For Peace to find
He harked behind
To hear the footfalls come
  Of those who walk
  But do not talk –
He were whilom as dumb.

With soft Despair:
  'They must be there.'
A zephyr stirred his cloak.
  'Alas, thereby
  No noise hear I!'
This cry aloud he spoke.

Flew back his words
  Like hoodless birds –
Echoed no other sound.
  Alack, 'twas true,
  To spy the two
He durst not turn around.

~

About the gentle, slow-treading god did stir
    No breeze. Illumed was he. – Lo,
One hand raised a staff, the other steadied: her!

The so-beloved, for whom arrives no fresh tomorrow,
    For whom the lyre brought forth such airs
In head-high waves of crashing sorrow

A new world then was born, a world of cares,
    No hues nor in its warp nor weft,
Of floorboards swept and, oh, abandoned chairs,

The days abashed, the lightless stars bereft,
    The world a world of blot and blur.
That so-beloved – dear ghost that sudden left.

~

    Great changes had she undergone –
        In thrall to Death thereby:
    Enripened; inward; meek-eyed; wan;
        Like one content to die.
    Apart she was, so scarce could stand
        The fair god's merest touch
    As forth he drew her by the hand –
        E'en that she deemed too much.

Tentative her tread, and slow,
    Restricted by her shroud;
Yet of that man ahead – her beaux,
    The gentle man she trowed
So well – nothing did she dream,
    Nor dreamt of, in that gloam,
The very track she trod nor any scheme
    To hie her home.

No more the woman dear to him
    In every song's refrain;
Henceforth a woman near to him
    As cloud to fallen rain;
Like long hair ribbon-loosed to fall
    Then stream with every gust
And gale; released was she withal.
    Already, she was dust.

And then the god stopped dead:
    'He's turned around!'
– No other word he said,
    Nor made a sound
And then let slip the woman's hand.
    What else to do?
She did not understand,
    But murmured only: 'Who?'

~

        – O whereupon
Afar, a figure shadow-black
Before the sunlit portal spied
      The god turn round
      Without a sound
      To follow her
   Already walking back
     Along that track.
     A distant blur,
  They moved then side by side –
The god, the woman dead.
    He watched them go.
    E'en though their tread
Tentative was, and slow,
    Soon they had gone.

The Edge of Sleep

There goes the light,
Leaving Rhossili Bay
Particulate grey –
And that's all right.
Nothing palls like white.
But should we stay
To watch the day
Turn into night?
Here, hand in hand,
While black waves flow
Across the sand?
In all this snow?
If we can't understand,
At least let us know.

So much snow
Coming to land
Where cold sheep stand
And wait. – Below,
The black waves flow
Across the sand
Like something planned.
. . . Time to go?
Time to walk away.
None too bright,
The sheep will stay
Another night,
Another day:
White on white.

Walking the Dead

                  into town
Then home before sundown;
Footsore, clock-watching.
Things left unsaid / Things said,
Strange traffic there, fresh signs
To follow: double yellow lines,
The light on buildings.

Kerbside with an *A-Z*
Unopened in no one's hand,
Who are we to understand
These streets' new leaves?
That blue overhead?

In My Other Life

blue as the blue of who knows what
the sky fills every window of my other life
and the marble hallway is lit by sunbeams
angled unlike any I have known

down shaded streets where traffic seldom strays
streets on which the day has opened like a song
the walk towards a square I may not reach
is all I need of happiness

and all of this and you are there
in my other life and the children as children
where a table is laid where the xeremies drone
and we stop in a passage of light

how good I am in my other life
how willing to believe and how awake
awake to all the tiles and air and stones
of which my other life is built

here is the bakery here is the church
and this is where I catch the tram (the rattly tram)
now where do I have to be?
and who will meet me at the other end?

A Portable Joye

And so the Boy unto himselfe
My handbagge doth procure

– With Lego, stickers, dolles
And bookes and yea with me

The others goe: my bunions
Toucheth not the ground!

Lo! Lanky shadowes growe
On shiny payving-stones,

Eftsoons a caravan of cloudlets
Crosseth yonder Heav'nly blue

And O! The playgrounde swings!
Whereby, mid golden leaves

And sunne, Boys riseth up!
But No! they crye, Not farre!

Not farre! – alonge his sleeve
The infante wipeth aye his snot

Then wondrous pastries passe
The corner of mine Eye,

The shopfrontes Ah! How wan!
How by the Summer faded!

Thence a smile, a regal wave
– Thank ye! Fare thee well!

Then onward we together goe
All armes but mine replete

The weighte?! I crieth – No!
They boome, No weighte at all,

Then crosseth we the road
And then you watche us goe

I AM JOYE!   I AM JOYE!
My children carry me

William Edward Knight
1921–2001

Helma Lydia Knight
1929–2019